D1716804

AMAZING SNAKES!

BUSH VIPERS

BY DAVY SWEAZEY

EPIC

BELLWETHER MEDIA • MINNEAPOLIS, MN

EPIC BOOKS are no ordinary books. They burst with intense action, high-speed heroics, and shadows of the unknown. Are you ready for an Epic adventure?

This edition first published in 2014 by Bellwether Media, Inc.

No part of this publication may be reproduced in whole or in part without written permission of the publisher. For information regarding permission, write to Bellwether Media, Inc., Attention: Permissions Department, 5357 Penn Avenue South, Minneapolis, MN 55419.

Library of Congress Cataloging-in-Publication Data

Sweazey, Davy.
  Bush Vipers / by Davy Sweazey.
    pages cm. – (Epic: Amazing Snakes!)
  Includes bibliographical references and index.
  Summary: "Engaging images accompany information about bush vipers. The combination of high-interest subject matter and light text is intended for students in grades 2 through 7"– Provided by publisher.
  Audience: Ages 7-12
  ISBN 978-1-62617-090-2 (hardcover : alk. paper)
  1. Atheris–Juvenile literature. I. Title.
  QL666.O69S94 2014
  597.96'3–dc23

                        2013034880

Printed in the United States of America, North Mankato, MN.

TABLE OF CONTENTS

WHAT ARE BUSH VIPERS?

Bush vipers are **venomous** snakes that live in bushes and trees. They grow up to 28 inches (70 centimeters) long. Bush vipers have short heads and thin necks.

Size Increase

Small, pointed scales cover their heads. Larger scales cover the rest of their bodies.

WHERE BUSH VIPERS LIVE

N
W E
S

bush viper range = ☐

Bush vipers live in the African **rain forest.**
Belly **scales** called **scutes** move them through trees.
They hold on to branches with their strong tails.

scutes

Bush vipers can have green, orange, or even blue scales. These colorful scales **camouflage** them.

True Colors
As bush vipers get older, their scales might completely change color!

BABY BUSHVIPERS

Female bush vipers give birth to around seven to nine baby snakes. Some babies have white tips on their tails. They wiggle the tip like a worm to attract prey.

Never Changing
Some types of bush vipers keep their white tail as adults!

HUNTING FOR PREY

Bush vipers smell with their mouths. They use their forked tongues to detect the scents of prey.

Bush
Viper
Prey

Bush vipers **ambush** small **rodents**, lizards, and birds. They hide until an animal comes close. Then they **strike**.

Bush vipers bite prey with special teeth called **fangs**. Venom flows through these teeth to kill the prey.

Folding Fangs

Bush vipers do not always show their fangs. The teeth can fold into the roof of the mouth.

Their **flexible** jaws stretch open wide. This helps bush vipers swallow prey whole!

SPECIES PROFILE

SCIENTIFIC NAME:	*ATHERIS*
COMMON NAMES:	USAMBARA EYELASH VIPER, WESTERN BUSH VIPER, HAIRY BUSH VIPER, MATILDA'S HORNED VIPER, GREAT LAKES BUSH VIPER, AFRICAN BUSH VIPER
AVERAGE SIZE:	15-28 INCHES (40-70 CENTIMETERS)
HABITAT:	RAIN FORESTS
RANGE:	WESTERN AND CENTRAL AFRICA
VENOMOUS:	YES
HUNTING METHOD:	AMBUSH, VENOMOUS BITE
COMMON PREY:	MICE, SHREWS, SMALL REPTILES, BIRDS

GLOSSARY

ambush—to attack by surprise

camouflage—to hide an animal or thing by helping it blend in with the surroundings

fangs—sharp, hollow teeth; venom flows through fangs and into a bite.

flexible—able to stretch

prey—animals that are hunted by other animals for food

rain forest—a hot, rainy area with tall trees

rodents—small animals that usually gnaw on their food

scales—small plates of skin that cover and protect a snake's body

scutes—large, rough scales on the stomach of a snake

strike—to bite quickly and with force

venom—a poison created by a snake; snakes use venom to hurt or kill other animals.

venomous—able to create venom in their bodies; bush vipers release venom through their teeth.

TO LEARN MORE

At the Library

McCarthy, Colin. *Reptile.* New York, N.Y.: DK Pub., 2012.

Stewart, Melissa. *Snakes!* Washington, D.C.: National Geographic, 2009.

Woodward, John. *Everything You Need to Know About Snakes: And Other Scaly Reptiles.* New York, N.Y.: DK Pub., 2013.

On the Web

Learning more about bush vipers is as easy as 1, 2, 3.

1. Go to www.factsurfer.com.

2. Enter "bush vipers" into the search box.

3. Click the "Surf" button and you will see a list of related Web sites.

With factsurfer.com, finding more information is just a click away.

INDEX

The images in this book are reproduced through the courtesy of: Biosphoto/ Daniel Heuclin, front cover, pp. 20-21; Willie Davis, p. 5; Biosphoto/ SuperStock, p. 7; David Northcott/ Danita Delimont/ Newscom, pp. 8-9; Steffen Foerster, pp. 10-11; Mark Kostich/ Getty Images, pp. 12-13; CreativeNature, p. 14 (top); EcoPrint, p. 14 (middle); Sue Robinson, p. 14 (bottom); agefotostock/ SuperStock, pp. 14-15; Andy Hunger/ Glow Images, pp. 16-17; Snowleopard1, pp. 18, 19.